JEN WEILAND

# Mz Cookie With Purpose

*The Story Behind The Why*

LiL PAC

People ➤ Attention ➤ Connection

Published by Lil Pac, LLC | W. Mansfield, Ohio 43358 | USA | [www.lilpac.com]

[Email at: hello@mzcookie.com]

First published in the United States by Lil Pac, LLC.

A Note from Mz. Cookie (Jen Weiland):

I'm not a therapist. I'm not a mental health professional. I'm a storyteller.

These stories are here to help you sit with what's true for you—not to "fix" you.

This is not therapeutic advice.

You matter. You're not too much. The world needs you in it.

Trigger Warning:

Some truths may stir up big feelings. That's okay. It's part of being human.

But if it feels like too much, please don't carry it alone.

You matter. You are not too much. You are needed.

Need someone to talk to?

988 Suicide & Crisis Lifeline (Available 24/7)

Call or Text: 988 | 988lifeline.org

Paperback ISBN: 979-8-9998211-2-6

EBook ISBN: 979-8-9998211-3-3

Thank you Reedsy!

First edition

ISBN: 979-8-9998211-2-6

This book was professionally typeset on Reedsy.
Find out more at reedsy.com

# Contents

# Disclaimer

Hello, my friend, and welcome.

Before we begin, a quick note. One piece of housekeeping to take care of.

**This is a work of creative nonfiction; real experiences are shared, but names and details have been adapted/changed for privacy.**

This book is drawn from real experiences and emotional truths.

To protect the privacy of individuals, some names and identifying details have been changed to honor privacy.

In a few cases, names remain the same with permission or are used symbolically.

These choices are made for storytelling purposes and do not necessarily represent literal or factual portrayals of those individuals.

Any resemblance to actual persons, living or deceased, is either coincidental or intentionally adapted for narrative purposes.

**This book is best understood as a work of creative nonfiction.**

Editing was done by the author. A professional editor was not retained for this work in order to preserve the author's natural voice. If you happen to notice a typo, feel free to reach out at **hello@mzcookie.com**. Thank you!

You can also follow the **MzCookieYouMatter Movement** by signing up for my newsletter at www.mzcookie.com. I'd love to stay connected with you.

# My Message to You

**The Lighthouse: From Broken to Beacon**

Sometimes the wound that shapes your life comes in a single sentence.

I was 13 when mine came.

Standing in that middle school hallway, my best friend turned to me and said: *"I don't want to be friends with you anymore. I don't like you. I never did."*

In that moment, shame carved its message into me: *You're not wanted.*

## The Mask We Learn to Wear

What's a 13-year-old supposed to do with emotions that big?

I did what many of us do. I hid. I built a mask to protect myself.

That mask got heavier with every forgotten birthday, every "you're too much," every rejection. By high school, people thought I was confident standing alone.

The truth? I was terrified.

I learned to fake it so well that no one saw the fear underneath. I isolated slowly so it wouldn't be noticed. I became an expert at pretending to be fine when I wasn't fine.

## When Faith Felt Like Another Performance

Even faith didn't erase the wound.

I heard church sermons about hope and love, but I also heard: *"Christians don't get depressed. If you do, you don't have enough faith."*

So I added another mask—faking faith. My messy, muddy version didn't look like everyone else's polished one.

I stood in a crowd of believers, completely alone, wondering if even God wanted me.

## The Deepest Darkness

By 32, the weight of shame was unbearable. Depression slammed into me like a tidal wave. Even with medical help, I drowned in the same message: *You're not wanted.*

I withdrew again. Only this time, it felt final.

I didn't reach out. I didn't want to burden anyone with my darkness. I wore my mask so well that no one knew how close I was to the edge.

## The Hand That Pulled Me Back

And then came a simple message from Trista, a young woman from church:
*"Hey Jen, there's this thing called Facebook. Can I send you a friend request?"*

Such a small gesture. But in my deepest isolation, it was a lifeline.

I stared at her message for days, afraid to respond. Afraid of rejection.

But finally, I asked myself: *What if this is someone who actually likes me?*

That friend request became the first crack of light pulling me out of the darkness.

## Finding My Purpose

Years later, my life coach, Keith, gave me words I'll never forget.

He said, *"You're like a lighthouse. The waves crash against you, but you stand, shining your light."*

The pain shaped me, but it didn't define me.

And suddenly, I saw my story differently. All those years I told others they mattered, all those cookies I baked and hands I reached out to—I was being the Trista someone else needed.

## The Message We All Need

Here's what I've learned: Hurt people hurt people. But healed people heal people.

If you're wearing a mask right now...

If you're hiding behind a smile at the table...

If you're pretending to be okay when you're not—I see you.

Because I was you.

You're allowed to not be okay. Your pain is real. Your hurt is heavy. And you matter—not despite it, but including it.

## To Those Who Ask, "How Did I Miss It?"

If you've lost someone and wonder, *"Why didn't they reach out?"* please hear this:

We get good at hiding. We isolate slowly so it won't show.

We smile for you because we love you, and we don't want to dim your joy with our darkness.

We don't reach out because we've already decided we're too much.

## A New Mission

Today, I'm writing the book I needed when I was 13. A book to tell kids, and adults, that their feelings aren't too big, too messy, or too broken.

My mission is simple: to be someone's Trista. To extend a hand. To sit with people in their pain without fixing. To remind them they're not broken—they're human.

## You Are the Light

So how do you help someone who's struggling?

Don't tell them they'll be fine, sit with them while they're not fine.

Don't rush them to heal, give them permission to feel.

And if *you* are the one struggling right now, remember this: you are not your pain.

You are the lighthouse. The waves will crash, that's what waves do. But waves don't define you. Your job is to keep shining. (*Thanks, Keith*).

The waves will always come. But you… you are a beacon.
**You matter. You belong. You are needed.**

So let me ask: Can I be your Trista today?
Can I whisper to you what I once needed someone to tell me?

**It's okay to not be okay. You are worth fighting for.**
**The light you carry matters more than you know.**

**You Matter to Me, and Yes… I will notice.**

www.mzcookie.com.

# Trigger Warning

Hello friend,

    I'm happy to see you here.

    Are you comfortable? I hope so.

    Can I pull up a seat beside you while you sit?

I don't want to fix you, but I want to give you a glimpse into my journey. Where I was at. The things I hide from everyone. Psst, they think I'm fine but the truth is, I hid behind that mask. Some days I still do.

I am not a therapist, so this is not medical advice. There are trained medical professionals in the world that will help you. I hope I help, but not from a therapist standpoint, yet from a personal standpoint.

Ahead through the pages is my story. The Why behind my mission and purpose. Some of what I share may stir up some pain in your own heart. You may see yourself in my story, or you may see someone you know.

For those, like me, that hide behind that mask, I apologize to you. It's our safe space, or hiding place and here I am going to share for others to see. To see us, where we are, where I was. How we hide. I'm sorry to ruin your trust in sharing, you can revoke my membership, yet I can't stand by any longer.

Mental health issues are something that I find difficult to talk about, and may be difficult for some to hear. I trust that my words meet you where ever you may be at. Whether they reflect your feelings and give you permission to feel "same" or that they may give you a little more understanding when you have the one that has gone silent.

Whichever place you are at, I hope to meet you in the moment.

I share my story not to stir emotions, yet to give you a place to sit. I hope that by the time you turn the last page that there is more understanding.

Hope.

And more freedom.

Yet as I share, I know the emotions and my story may make it difficult for you in your moment. Can I ask you something? If it gets to be too much, can you put the book down. Wait a little moment while the words allow you a place to be. The book will be here for later when you are stronger. It's okay. My story isn't to stir up pain, yet I know this may be painful. It was painful for me to come out of hiding this journey to share.

If it feels like it is too much, I ask you to do two things for me.

Don't go it alone. Don't go into hiding like I did. Reach out and talk to someone.

I know, this is a hard request to ask of you. I've been in that spot, afraid of being labeled. Afraid of staying stuck. Afraid that someone wouldn't understand. It took me a great while before I found my life coach, Keith. But I did find someone to sit with me. And I know there is someone in the world ready to sit with you.

It's scary talking to someone about how you really feel. Those emotions are scary. the thoughts that spin. The questions of if you matter (which you do, to me). But you're allowed to feel them.

I have one more requests. Okay maybe a moment of begging. Can you please give it one more day?

I'm selfish to ask that of you for a personal reason.

I didn't want to give it one more day. I was at my end. I had given up. But do you know what happened when I gave it one more day. I was rescued. I wasn't healed, but I was given hope. I hope that through this story it also gives you hope. Courage to see how much you're needed. That you belong. That you matter.

There's a weird thing about this hope stuff, though. It didn't come to me in a way that I thought it would. In how I wanted it to look. What I thought it should look like.

When it came to me, I almost missed it.

And in my journey, the rescuing has changed.

I gave it one more day, and here I am sharing with you. Not to heal you, yet to give you a hand, a hope, and a whisper...I see you, I was once there, can you give me one more day?

I would say I'm still not healed from the wounds, yet I am different. And different is okay.

Many of my friends and family didn't know where I was at. I got very good at hiding from them. I sit here today, with you, not hiding from you. I see you and I feel your pain with you. You matter to me, which I know is hard to believe when the world has told you otherwise. But you really do, you matter to me. You don't have to believe what I say right now, yet I hope one day you see it.

My two requests:
    Don't go it alone.
    Give it one more day.

It's okay to not be okay, you're normal. And one day you will be different. Your pain changes you, and that's okay.

# The Mz. Cookie You Matter Movement

Ahead is the story behind the mission. It's what I will be doing to change a life. As you will read, my life was changed by someone who reached out to me.

Will you join me to reach out to others?

Where do I find the book so I can be a part of the **Mz Cookie You Matter Movement?**
    The book in paperback is available on Amazon.
    Order extra copies or mail one to a friend.
    You don't have to know where they are at, just tell them **They Matter.**

The link to Amazon is
    https://a.co/d/33Rzm1c

Or if that does not work search:
    **Mz Cookie You Matter** in the search box on Amazon.

I'm not a tech wiz, and I'm doing this tech stuff by the seat of my pants. Forgive me for the errors, yet I do know that on the Amazon search, you will find the book.

And from the www.mzcookie.com website, you can click to the Amazon store.

You can follow the story as we grow, also on my website
    at www.mzcookie.com

Join the newsletter where I will share and celebrate you.

Together, we can give them one more day.

**They Matter. This Matters. You Matter.**

# My Story: From Wound to Lighthouse

## A Question I Wonder About

Have you ever looked at a stranger in a restaurant and wondered what their life is like?

I wonder about that.

Why? Because I see myself in that booth. Alone, yet amongst friends or family. And I wonder, are they sitting where I was at? Pretending to be fine while sitting with a hurt. A hurt I couldn't share because my emotions were too much for someone else to handle.

I was sitting in a hiccup and struggling in my own life, and nobody knew. My heart ached as I pasted the "I'm fine" across my face. A "don't let them know what I'm feeling because I can't handle more pain in this moment, and if I talk about it, I will come undone."

The "I'm fine" mask. The one I carried well when I was having a little hiccup in life. Do you ever wonder who else is wearing that same mask?

Right now, someone is sitting alone, carrying a hurt they can't name. Maybe it's the person at table six picking at their food, or the server who keeps checking her phone. Maybe it's you.

We all have moments where we wonder: "Do I matter? Does anyone see me?"

## The Beginning of My Pain

I was 13 when it happened.

My first heart-shattering hurt. A wound that I started to filter life and experiences through. A painful moment that shaped my life.

I was 32 when the pain started to shift. A random request. An extended hand. A hope.

## Eighth Grade Hallway

At 13, a shattering pain echoed in my heart that changed so much of my life. My best friend told me she didn't want to be my friend anymore. No warning, no signals to prepare me for that moment. I stood in the hallway at school as she walked away, trying not to cry and trying not to let go of all the pieces of my heart.

My mind was confused. What happened? What did I do wrong? Why doesn't she like me? What's wrong with me?

Past the confused mind of me at 13, it was my heart that was confused. It wasn't only the heart-shattering moment of being told I wasn't worth someone being friends with—it was the shame that crept into my heart. It wasn't only the words, it was the feeling that came with it.

Shame.

This wasn't the first time I felt I wasn't wanted. I had other moments before this that hurt my little heart and emotions. Other moments, I had cried, "nobody wants to play with me" and "nobody wants to be my friend."

This one was different. She was my first friend outside of family and neighbors. What I felt was a connection to a "stranger" who chose to like me. Someone not in proximity to location or family.

I don't know, maybe I was weird with her, and I latched onto a hope that someone would like me.

We spent summers together, days and weeks at a time. We called each other, wrote to each other. During school, we hung out together. We shared secrets and stories, hopes and dreams.

What we wanted to be when we grew up. The boys we liked. The smelly teachers and the bleachers. Our favorite foods at lunch.

I was blindsided by her announcement. It was the end of the school year. A few of us roaming the halls and then her announcement.

She turned around and told me...

Her words: "I don't want to be friends with you anymore. I don't like you, I never did."

For the first time, I felt I wasn't wanted at a level that was beyond my family and neighbors not wanting to hang out with me because they told me they didn't like me.

Everything from that moment was filtered through that shame. That rejection. The shame of hearing "you're not wanted."

What was I supposed to do? How was I supposed to feel with this big emotion?

This was the beginning of my biggest question in life: "Do I matter?"

## Learning to Hide

By the time I got home from school, I had figured out how to stuff that emotion. I didn't want to talk about what hurt and how much it hurt. I was in my shame of not being wanted, and I felt that if I told anyone, they would confirm that feeling. Or make it worse.

I didn't want to feel worse, so I hid. I isolated. I covered up the wound.

I thought that it was the healthy way to handle it. Yet now I see, in covering the wound, it festered.

And I filtered.

Every experience from that moment was filtered through her words.

It wasn't the first time I had heard I wasn't wanted, but it was my most painful moment.

It was the end of the school year, and I had all summer to decide how I was going to go on from there. At the end of summer, it would be time to head into my freshman year of high school. I had given myself a task through the summer to practice protecting myself.

It's when I learned to wear the mask. A mask to protect me. A mask made heavier by the shame that stirred in my heart.

A few years ago, I ran into a fellow who was in my class. He had told me that I was the oddest one in our class because I stood alone. I didn't fit in with any one group, yet somehow was a part of the class. I stood by myself during high school.

I didn't try to be friends with anyone, but I was friendly to everyone. He then told me that he had the biggest crush on me because he thought it was cool - I could stand by myself like that.

Oh, Bruno, if you only knew.

## More Wounds, Deeper Shame

Let's fast forward past a lot of ups and downs and more moments that compounded the theme I kept hearing in my heart: "You're not wanted." Let's just say, there were many, many moments that I decided to stuff those feelings and bury them under the shame that kept growing. Forgotten birthdays, being told I wasn't liked, being told I was too much, and having proof that I wasn't liked.

Even in spite of my best efforts to be nice to people, I still wasn't liked.

I had heard this from others, and then I had a moment that piled one more shame feeling on my already heavy load that made me sink the furthest that I had ever felt.

## The Estate Discovery - Another Layer of "You're Not Wanted"

Fast forward a few decades, and my husband and I experienced the loss of a family member. Throughout the estate process, we discovered some information and another sting. In the paperwork, we realized how much I wasn't liked. I had suspected it, yet nothing was verified until after death.

Again, the wound of "You're not wanted" opened again.

I stood there listening to what was being said in the discovery. Trying not to come undone as I was feeling not just my pain, yet my husband's as well.

I reached out with my emotions wide open, hurt and devastated. Feeling selfish for allowing myself to feel this pain. Knowing how to carry my husband's pain, yet not knowing how to carry my own.

I was trying to carry the pain for my husband while trying to cover up the pain from a deep wound that he didn't know was there. He didn't know the wound was there, and I felt shame at that moment for how I was feeling.

I didn't handle this moment well. I was trying to deny and cover my own pain, yet it hurt.

Thirty-two years by this time of a constant message "you're not wanted" didn't feel temporary. It was suffocating and I was drowning.

And once again, I isolated.

## The Doctor's Wisdom

Well, somewhat. The doctor put me on medicine to help my mind and body heal, as she said. She had known I was dealing with depression prior to my visit. She was just waiting for me and for this moment. She had one request for me with the medicine: talk to someone about my emotions. Allow someone to listen to what I was feeling so they could help me. The medicine plus therapy—that was her solution.

Three therapy sessions later, well, I had to make a decision. Do I allow the pain to be compounded by being told "it's a temporary feeling, you'll feel better, you'll be fine"? Or do I go it alone because I felt they didn't understand and I hated to be labeled?

Any guesses which way I went?

Yup, a normal pattern—I isolated.

Therapy was making me feel worse, and I was spinning. I didn't understand my emotions, and I was getting my legs knocked out every session.

Back to my doctor, it was time to adjust the medicine.

She allowed me the space to be brave when I told her that therapy wasn't helping yet—it was making me feel worse. She allowed me the space without judgment.

She extended a little wisdom: find something to do that soothes my heart, and be okay if people don't understand why it helps you.

So that's what I did. I found something to soothe my heart while I remained isolated from the world.

## Faith and More Wounds

Now, if you can give me permission to share a small picture of where I was in this moment.

At age 18, my soon-to-be husband and I were going through pre-marital counseling. We were told it would be a benefit to our marriage (29 years later, I would agree). I found God during one of those sessions. After our wedding, we started to attend the church a little more.

Did attending the church give me immunity from the pain and the healing to the wound? I'd like to say yes, but it didn't. Some days, it made things feel worse.

I don't share that to cast judgment on churches. And I didn't grasp what was happening until we were attending a service at another church as guests and that pastor shared something profound: "More often than not, church is the one place where the congregation shoots their own wounded."

I don't share that to allow you space to point more accusations at the churches, yet for an understanding. Hurt people hurt people. And hurt people are found in whatever setting it may be.

Whether at a church, a sporting event, a restaurant, a family gathering, a festival, or in rush hour traffic. Hurt people are everywhere, hiding in plain sight amongst us.

Here I am sitting and absorbing what Pastor Steve is saying and giving myself permission to grieve at the same time. The one place I was told I would feel safe, where hope and love is supposed to be, I was finding more pain. I was listening to the words "There's hope here. There's love here. There's peace here." Yet my wound and pain from 13-year-old me was still open and raw.

And the shame that I felt at 13 was still there. My thoughts and feelings still stirring. My "why am I not healing if this is the place to heal?"

And the "You're a Christian and Christians aren't depressed, and if they are, that is proof they don't trust God."

Here I am, standing in my pain and my shame and listening

to someone tell me that I wasn't a real Christian because I was depressed and anxious. Here I am feeling like God doesn't even want me. Being told that I need to serve others.

Being told I had to perform to find my way into His grace and me standing there with a hurt that I couldn't name and an emotion that was too big for me to handle. An emotion that was growing because of the shame of me failing.

I thought I was in a safe place, yet I was getting shot at.

Once again, I isolated.

I don't share this to cast judgment on the church. It is what it was. A place where hurt people gather together in hope and community. A place to belong.

Yet I didn't belong. I carried it silently that God didn't love me the way He loved everyone else there. They didn't have the wound I had, I didn't look like them. I didn't think like them. I didn't feel like them. I was alone amongst a lot of people within the walls of a church.

And I was spinning further down.

Again, the wound that I filtered everything through was showing me that even in a church I wasn't wanted.

It wasn't until I heard Pastor Steve share his profound wisdom before I could understand. Yes, he says "church is where we shoot our own wounded" but I see this happen everywhere.

Not just at church.

So now you know another layer to the shame that was growing. Trying to be someone I wasn't because I was labeled a Christian.

Can I share a truth with you if you are sitting in that same pain? Being a Christian and feeling you are not allowed to feel pain because you're told "that's not being a Christian because you feel like that. Where is your faith?"

This is what I learned, a lot later, but a truth I learned.

I call it faith, not to avoid the pain, yet to feel it.

To give yourself permission to be human. To give yourself permission to go to God in whatever state you are in. He doesn't call us to be perfect. And He is okay that we aren't perfect. And He is okay that we feel things the way we feel them.

Feeling them doesn't mean that we don't have faith.

I had believed that I had to come to God without blemish and free from pain. It took me a long time to realize that I was allowed to go to Him in whatever state I was feeling.

How I saw others walk their faith, I tried to do the same.

I tried not to be afraid. I tried to be confident. I tried to do everything they told me to do which I felt that God would love me.

I came into my relationship with God broken and I heard other Christians tell me that to be a Christian I had to do it a certain way and feel a certain way. The more I tried, the more my own shame made me feel like I was failing.

I was being shot at and shooting myself.

And the hardest one I carried: "You're a Christian, Christians aren't depressed or anxious and if they are they have no faith."

Here I am living in the shame that I have no faith because I was depressed.

Again, I learned to get stronger by carrying that mask.

I had to fake who I was so I wouldn't be shamed.

I had to fake being happy so I wouldn't hear the judgment.

I had to fake being okay when I wasn't okay.

Because I was a Christian I had to cover up and hide.

I had to fake my faith to look like theirs.

If they knew where I was at, am I going to get shot again?

I didn't want to get shot again, so I faked it.

That's the beauty of learning how to carry the mask—you get really good at faking it around others. Don't let them know.

They don't care to know.

The truth: I had faith but it didn't look like theirs.

My faith was muddy and messy, yet it was there.

Being in church made my messy messier and my shame, it grew much bigger.

And I hope that by sharing this, that you, my friend, will see that I was standing there, amongst other Christians with a broken heart trying to cover a pain.

I was standing there in a crowd, alone and broken.

And if you're standing in that same space right now, can I tell you something?

It's okay to hurt. It's okay to feel pain. It's okay to carry that mask.

I see you standing there and I stand there with you.

I feel this with you and I want to whisper to your heart:

You're allowed.

That pain you're feeling, it's real.

The hurt you're holding, it's heavy.

Will you let me carry it with you?

Will you let me sit with you?

Will you allow me to whisper to your heart, you're not broken, you're normal and it's okay you're not okay?

I'm still not okay some days. Did you know that's part of all of this?

I still have moments where I feel heavy. Where things get flipped upside down.

I have lost hope in complete healing.

Why? Because I had a moment where I gave myself permission.

I gave myself permission in that I will visit that pain again and again. And I'm allowed.

Are things better for me today?

Nope.

But things are different.

I had a friend guide me in this truth. Keith had shared about his journey with me and he shared a message that changed my thoughts:

"Every song sounds a little different, it depends on how you tune into it."

How do I translate that? The pain and the shame from my wound will sound a little different every time it comes up. It depends on how I tune into it.

I would love to lay the shame down, yet if I am honest, much of my life was filtered through that first "you're not wanted" moment.

Will it heal completely? I don't know.

But I know now, every time it comes up it sounds a little different now.

How? Because I gave myself permission to be okay with not being okay with it. The hurt happened to me and it has defined so much of my life...my song. But that hurt isn't me.

## The Deepest Isolation

I put on the mask "I'm fine" because by this moment, I knew that people didn't understand the emotions I was feeling. I avoided conversations because I didn't want their words to add more to the heavy load I was carrying. I isolated.

I started to not go around my friends and group settings. Events and functions where my friends were. Carrying the mask of "I'm fine" was heavy and exhausting, and I didn't have the capacity to carry the pain and the mask.

Here is the thing. I isolated slowly from everyone. They didn't notice, they were busy living their lives while I was busy dealing with a pain that I couldn't heal. A pain that I didn't know how to cover up.

Then the isolation compounded further. I realized that my friends didn't notice I was missing. The pain and wound I was trying to heal was starting to grow. It was becoming a weapon. Those thoughts I was having were starting to repeat faster and faster. I was spinning and I couldn't stop it.

My internal thoughts in every situation: "See, here we are again, they are showing me how I don't matter. Why try? They don't even notice that I'm not there. They exclude me. See, this is proof that I'm not wanted."

When I was in my "Do I matter" moment I was quite low. And low enough I was isolated and didn't want to find help.

When I went to the stores and work, I didn't interact with anyone and I carried the thoughts with me "Why am I here, I don't matter, no one notices me." No interaction, no eye contact, no smiles, no words. I was lost in the emotions of my own isolation.

## A Lesson from the ER - Why We Don't Reach Out

Can I share a story about the pain of being labeled? Labeled by our family, friends and the establishment. A label that can terrorize the heart and grow the wound even wider.

My husband had to take a trip to the emergency room, a kidney stone had decided to launch its way to the exit and then got stuck. I'm sitting with him awaiting the time the ER could get a room ready for him.

The doors open and along with the deputy a young man. Both standing waiting for their turn to talk with the admissions clerk. The young man was shifting, the deputy's voice quiet. A lot was being spoken by the body language that words weren't capturing.

A few moments later the young man's mother comes into the waiting room. He is back in a private room to finish registration. She speaks to the deputy words that hurt me as I listened.

The deputy is shifting as his mother shares a painful hurt, "He's doing it to get attention. I don't understand why he's so emotional. He said he needed to talk, but he's doing all of this for attention. He just needs to listen to you and the doctors, but he doesn't want to listen."

The young man doesn't hear his mother's words to the deputy. The deputy doesn't say much other than "He's here so we can get him some help."

I'm sitting there picking up the pain in this moment. An unspoken pain.

The young man comes out of the room back to the waiting area. The deputy is now talking to the registration staff to see if they are able to get a room ready quicker. He's trying to get the young man help in a space that can help him.

The young man sits down, fidgeting and his body language shows he is scared and uncertain. Not saying much until the mother hits the wound with her words and he reacts. She keeps telling him to listen to people, to get help, that he's doing this for attention.

In the moment, where she hits the wound, he responds. "I just needed you to listen, I needed to talk. You are blowing this all out of the water. You calling the deputy, now I'm losing everything. My house, my wife, my family and because you wouldn't give me the time to tell you how I was feeling. You chose to call the deputy and now I'm labeled. I'm labeled for life. I wanted to talk and now you got me labeled."

The pain in those words "labeled" I picked up.

In this situation I realized why I myself didn't reach out for help. From a friend, or family, or doctors, or the system designed to help us and save us. That label.

Not just the label in their paperwork and diagnosis. But the unspoken labels that swirl around someone having an emotional moment.

A brief moment with a lifetime sentence – that label.

His words echo in my heart: "I just needed you to listen. I needed to talk and now, now I'm labeled for life."

That word — labeled — is this why so many stay silent...

A brief moment of emotion becomes a lifetime sentence.

This is why I didn't reach out. Even though the pain grew, I was having a moment in life that I couldn't get out of, yet I didn't want a permanent label tied to my moment.

That label told a story about my entire life while I was having a moment. A label that would stay with me years after I came out of the one moment.


## For Those Left Behind


Now why do I share this, the isolating slowly part? Being labeled?

Because I am on the other side of losing friends. Four friends. Four people I've known that I didn't know where they were at in their emotions. And they made a permanent decision.

Four friends who needed permission to hurt without the terror of being labeled for life.

Four friends who needed someone to sit in the mud with them without judgment.

And I see that I was in that same spot. I was in that same space. And I can see how it's missed. And I can hear the questions of those left behind to pick up the pieces.

The questions they ask: "How did I not know?" and "Why didn't they reach out?"

Can I answer those two questions?

The first—how did you not know? For me, many didn't know where I was at because of the mask I wore and I learned to do the isolating slowly. I suspect some may have known where I was at, but the past pain I carried taught me to hide it. That my emotions were too big for some to carry. That sometimes the best intentions of hearing "you'll be fine, this is temporary" made the pain worse.

It's not an accusation on them. I know it was intended to cheer me up. But it didn't. That "temporary" pain I was told would pass, in that moment it didn't feel temporary. And I didn't feel like I was going to be fine.

What I needed was a moment for someone to listen, without judgment and without hurrying me up. I wasn't okay and didn't feel okay and I needed someone to sit with me, not to fix me.

I wonder if that is the heavy burden others carry into their isolation much like I did.

And being told I would be fine.

Well, I didn't feel fine.

I was messy and that feeling I was carrying was big. I didn't know how to handle it. And I learned to not share because others couldn't handle that pain. Maybe it's because it stirred a wound in their own hearts and it scared them too. I don't know. I can't speak to their emotions. I share where I was at.

Now I may have answered the second question, why didn't they reach out. But can I expand on that a little more?

The why they didn't reach out. I can't speak for the ones that I have lost. Or the ones that also hid behind the mask, pretending to be fine. Much like I have done.

But here is why I didn't reach out. Two different things were happening. Two things that kept me from sharing.

The simple answer: the very few moments I did, I may have shared with the wrong person at that time. Someone not capable of helping me heal because they had their own wound and when I shared it brought pain to their hearts as well. A pain they tried to cover and hide and my emotions stirred in them something they didn't want to face again.

My pain may have stirred their pain.

The other reason why I didn't reach out:

To put it simpler, I saw the joy they were having in their life and I didn't want to take that away by sharing where I was at. I saw how they were doing these fun things and sharing their fun adventures. Telling me about the wonderful things they were doing. They were living life. They were busy. They were living the dream. Doing fun things. I was listening to their joy and all the things they were doing.

And here I am stuck in the mud. I was genuinely happy for them. I loved seeing them live life.

And I also put myself behind that mask further.

I told myself: Don't share, they are too busy. Don't share, they are having a moment of joy. Don't share, I don't want to take away their moment.

Don't share, they don't have time for me.

In this cycle, I got really good at hiding my pain. Living behind that mask. I figured out what others wanted to hear. What others wanted to see. What others were saying about those who they found out were dealing with depression.

I used all of that information to put up walls. I didn't want to be labeled the way they labeled everyone else. I listened to what they said and I adapted. I adjusted.

I wore that mask. And I suspect others wear that same mask.

I wonder when I see the one sitting in the corner at the

restaurant, you know the quiet one pretending to smile and fit in.

I wonder about them. The mask they wear.

And I see myself in them. Sitting amongst friends yet feeling alone.

Listening to what they share, afraid to tell anyone how heavy things feel at the moment.

So to go back and answer the questions: "How did I not know?" and "Why didn't they reach out?"

The bigger answer is if they are like me, we do things on purpose so you don't know.

We do what we do because we don't want you to know.

We know you love us, yet in that moment we don't love ourselves.

We know you mean well when you tell us that it will be okay. We don't trust when you tell us that because in that moment, things aren't okay.

The thoughts we think and feel, yes they scare you, yet they also scare us too.

We learn how to cope until it becomes unbearable. And we know that you are left with the questions and the whys. We feel that with you.

Would you allow me to circle back to something about how we get so good at covering up what we are feeling?

This isn't to cast judgment, yet to open a conversation.

One thing that taught me to hide was when I heard others say, "They are just trying to get attention. They aren't serious. They are doing it for attention."

Can I ask you to understand something?

When that person's heart is so heavy that they do ask for help and are met with a comment like that—whether to their face or behind their back—that can be what makes or breaks someone on giving it one more day.

What I suspect is that those that say, "they are doing it for attention," may be dealing with is fear. So words can be spoken out of fear.

For me, I didn't hear the fear. I heard the judgment and hid myself even further.

It is scary to have those thoughts and feelings: "What's the point. Why am I even here. Would anyone notice if I'm gone. Nobody cares."

It's scary for you to hear that. And it's scary for us to feel that.

And this is one way that I almost slipped through that crack and left my family with those same questions.

I heard it spoken about others. The accusation that they were doing it for attention.

Can I correct that thought? It's not for attention. It is a real hurt. A hurt that doesn't heal and it makes the mind wonder: Why am I here? What is the point?

And that hurt pushes the feelings to a decision.

If someone reaches out and shares those feelings, can I ask you to do something? Don't come at them telling them it will be okay. Because in that moment, it doesn't feel it will be okay. And don't lump them into the stereotype that they are doing it for attention. It's a hurt that needs healed, not a way to get attention.

For those in that emotion and feeling the way they do and then hearing those say those things—this is why it gets missed. It got missed with my family and my friends.

I heard them say things, and here I was in those same hopeless emotions. Hearing what was said, I learned how to cover it up. I used those accusations on others to change how I did things.

I was more afraid of being labeled. The stigma around that label.

This is how it gets missed.

Now this isn't a judgment, this is coming from someone on the other side sharing with an open heart to help you understand.

To help those that hide to understand, I see you where you are and I understand why you hide. I did it too. I was afraid of being labeled as too much. Labeled as trying to get attention.

When what I needed was to have someone listen. Much like the heart cry from that young man in the ER.

To those who don't understand where that person is at, I hope this helps. I may not ever heal your wound from your loss, but I hope it helps you understand.

It's not you, it's us in that moment. We have an emotion too big and too heavy for us to carry and being labeled makes us hide from you.

## Where My Story Changes

But where my story changes.

Where I had a crack of hope that started to rewrite the message my wound was sending to my identity.

At my lowest, I had a random moment.

At this time, I had already closed myself off from everyone I knew. I slowly stopped going to church. I slowly stopped hanging out with friends. I slowly stopped calling my friends.

I slowly isolated and chose for myself to be alone in my hurt.

Until one day, I got a message.

A young lady from the church reached out to me. The message was simple: "Hey Jen, there's this thing called Facebook, and I was wondering if you were on there and if I could send you a friend request."

Out of the blue, a random message. A random request.

I sat in that for a few days. I didn't want to do it. I didn't want to set myself up to be rejected and open that wound I still carried from eighth grade. I was standing there in her message as my 13-year-old self. I didn't want to relive that pain.

And then I asked a question: "What if this is someone who does like me?"

I waited a few days. I wasn't sure.

Before this moment, I had a few experiences where I thought that someone wanted to be my friend. I allowed myself to think I was likable by someone and yet the situation wasn't what I thought it was. They wanted the use of me, not the friend of me. Something else that fed my hurt, "You're not wanted."

At the time, I didn't know there were people who existed that wanted me, not the use of me.

I decided to go slow with the Facebook thing. I didn't want to hurt again.

I looked at the message from Trista again and again. A little glimmer of hope: "What if someone did like me?"

A random person, extending a hand.

A random person, she made me feel like I mattered for a moment.

A random invitation that started to heal a wound I couldn't carry.

The moment I decided to give it one more day. The moment I had a hope.

## Thirty-Five Years Later

I know the expert academics tell me not to bounce around when I share a story, yet I want to bounce this one forward. Forward 16 years to where I am now.

Sixteen years from that invite to be someone's friend on a thing called Facebook.

Sixteen years from the moment Trista gave me a reason to give it one more day.

You remember how I told you I learned how to carry a mask and fake it. A mask that was created when I was 13. One I learned to use to hide from people so they wouldn't see and wouldn't label.

Now, as I sit and share this with you, I am 48. This, 16 years after Trista. This, 35 years of not understanding the whole story. Thirty-five years from the heart-shattering moment of me at 13. Wondering what was wrong with me, why someone didn't like me. Wondering if I mattered. Wondering if anyone would notice. Wondering if anyone cared.

Wondering if I was a friend to anyone.

At my lowest, I think back and I see the moment that turned my life around.

The Trista, that reached out a hand to ask me to be her friend on this Facebook world.

She didn't know where I was at.

She didn't need to know.

And up until a few days ago I didn't realize it was her that actually saved me.

Saved me from being a statistic.

Saved my family and friends from asking those questions and picking up the pieces.

She allowed me a small moment to put my mask down. For a moment. I let myself believe that someone out there liked me and that I mattered to someone.

Where do these thoughts come from?

I found a new "therapist"—well he is a life coach by title. But I found more in him and his wisdom than in any other coach. He saw me behind the mask I was carrying. He heard me past the words I was using. He heard what I was saying, what I was feeling and he didn't push to fix me. He pushed to allow me to let him sit with me.

He sat with me.

He sat with me in what I was feeling and why I was stuck.

I know there are some negative thoughts around seeing someone in the therapy world. Yet I am thankful he didn't have the credentials behind his name that would have kept me from reaching out.

His bio on Spring Health shared how he himself dealt with emotions and what he did in those moments. His bio made me feel like I was seen before he ever met me. His bio gave my emotions space.

Where he was in chapter two, I felt he could help guide me out of the chapter one I was perpetually stuck in. But, I didn't know what was keeping me stuck until most recent.

Through the many conversations and him challenging my thoughts and feelings, he opened my eyes to my story. A story I have buried. A story with many pieces and many people that helped build my story.

He also challenged my fears. He allowed me to lean into why I was feeling as much as I was. He didn't push to fix. He sat with me to help me feel.

I suspect he knows that the stuck we get stuck in is partly fear and partly the story we tell ourselves around the events that happened.

## The Lighthouse Revelation

In our last, most recent chat, he shared with me something that challenged my life of thoughts.

He told me where I am in my moment, I am a lighthouse. The waves that crash against a lighthouse are what they are. Waves. Waves doing what waves do.

He didn't ask me to do this, but I took what he said and I sat in it. Considering a thought that I was allowed to be a lighthouse. A moment, and a choice to give myself permission to be that I am. Doing that which is me. Standing as I stood. And naming the pain, the waves.

As I sat in the thoughts about the waves and the lighthouse, more thoughts came to my heart. It was heavy, it felt weird, it was my permission.

The waves and pain of my past shaped me. They are what they are. They did what they did.

I flashed back to moments of my past that hurt. Those wounds that shaped me. I felt the pain of the wave, the impact.

And then I looked with different eyes to see there amongst the hardest hitting waves, there were gentle ones. Ones that called to me in peace.

And I saw for the first time, the one that called to me in peace. The one, this Trista, that called to me that pulled me out.

Remember when I shared that my doctor also encouraged me to find something that brought me joy and to protect it?

Here's where I see the picture grow wider.

Three years after Trista asked me to join her in the Facebook world, I found more people that liked me. And more people that didn't like me (hello, that unfriend button hurts).

Three years later, the thing that brought me joy turned into a business. And a mission. But until now, I didn't see the mission I was on during my business days.

And I didn't see any of this until Keith shared about the lighthouse.

## The Mission I Didn't Know I Was On

Would you allow me to zoom out?

Until now, I didn't realize that it was more than cookies I was baking. I was serving a message "You matter" through every order and every interaction.

I strived to show people how much they mattered to me. How much I needed them.

Why?

Because that was what I needed for so many years.

To hear someone say, "Hey Jen, you matter." I was saying that to every order.

I was to those who I met as Trista was to me when she asked me to join Facebook with her.

But I didn't see all of that until now.

Other than Keith opening my eyes, what else happened?

A book…

I had a moment during this unsticking my stuck time where I isolated myself again. But it was for a different reason.

I had words to share. I had a story in my heart to harvest.

As I sat in that moment, my heart poured out onto the pages.

Thinking about myself where I was at 13. An emotion so heavy I didn't know how to carry.

And then all the other emotions I had felt through my 35 years of moments. Moments filtered by that pain. That heart-shattering moment.

I sat in my feelings, not knowing that this would be my own lighthouse.

I sat in what had happened naming the waves that crashed against me all of my life.

I named what it was and what it felt like.

When I came out of the other side of all of wave naming moments, I reached out to Keith again. With a bigger pain. And a wondering.

What if I had this book in eighth grade…

What if I had someone sit with me in my emotions…

What if I had someone to sit with me, not to fix it yet to just sit with me…

Would my life have been different?

Could it make a difference in someone else's life?

Could I use it for a mission, much like I did in business, to show people they aren't too much; they matter?

Could I be a lighthouse to someone out there that needs to be seen?

Much like Trista reached out and it started to pull me out of my darkness, could I do the same to someone else?

Could I change a child's story?

I look back and I see where I was, standing in the hallway, listening to the words "I don't want to be your friend anymore." And dealing with the emotions of not being wanted.

And I zoom into that child standing in the hallway holding their hurt. Could I help change their story?

And then I look at those sitting in the restaurant, wondering if they are quiet because they don't have someone to hold their pain.

Or the young man that is dealing with the emotions, being told to be someone he is not. Can I help him see who he is and how much he matters?

And then my thoughts go to the four I have lost. And I think:

If I could have been a Trista to them, could I have made a

difference?

Could I have given them space to be while they were hiding in their pain?

## The Permission I Wish I Could Have Given

What words would I say if I were standing in the mud with someone right now, looking them in their eyes, hand outstretched?

A permission slip to hurt.

A gentle word that says, "I see your mask of 'I'm fine' and it is heavy. Let me help you carry it."

I'm saying "Stop. Sit with me. What you're feeling is real, it's valid, and you don't have to carry it alone."

That permission slip I needed in eighth grade - that's what could have changed everything.

Not "it gets better" (though it does).

Not "think positive" (though that helps).

Just: "It's okay that this hurts. You're not broken for feeling this way. The hurt doesn't make you too much."

This movement isn't about solving people's problems - it's about giving them permission to feel their feelings without shame.

The restaurant stranger who gets the book and reads "It's okay to not be okay" - maybe that's the first time anyone's told them that.

The kid who gets TaterTot's message before they build walls around their heart - maybe they learn early that feeling deeply isn't a character flaw.

The parents watching their child pull away - maybe the book helps them say "I see you hurting, and that's okay. You don't have to protect me from your pain."


## Why This Book Exists - For the Eighth Grader


I know, you see this book listed on Amazon and it says it's for the 6-16 year olds. Yet, I wrote this for everyone, no matter the age.

So why target this age group? I think about that moment for myself in eighth grade. My first wound that life filtered through.

Why this book says it's for 6-16 years old?

Because that is when I experienced my first emotional wound and I didn't heal it. I didn't know how to name that moment. I stood there shattered, my first rejection.

A wound that walked around with me and kept growing.

And I think: What if I can help your child in that moment when they feel their first rejection? Their first moment of grief. Their first moment of shame.

I think about where I was when I was in eighth grade. Standing with a shattered heart, wondering what was wrong with me. Why I wasn't lovable.

And I wonder...if I had this book, how much different my life would have been.

How I could have learned what that emotion I was feeling really was and learned how to talk to myself. Could I have been saved from the painful moments that fed my wounds and thoughts that I wasn't wanted?

I think about that and then think about your child.

And the moment I didn't go to my own mom because it hurt so bad and I didn't want her to carry that pain too. I knew she'd carry it with me, but I didn't want to make her hurt. My little mind didn't understand that my mom already knew what it felt like. All I saw was that my mom would also carry that pain with me. And I was trying to protect her from feeling what I was feeling.

I think about your child in that moment and then I think of you, the parent. Not understanding why they aren't talking about it. Knowing something happened yet met with their silence.

Their guard up.

Not letting you in.

And you standing on the sidelines, patiently waiting for them to open to you. You carrying a different hurt seeing your child pull away from you. Not knowing what to say while you're holding their heart.

I think of you as a parent, feeling lost and wanting to reach your child in their moment and yet being gentle and giving them space.

That's why this book exists.

I think about myself, holding my shattered heart, afraid to hurt my mom yet not knowing I needed someone to sit with me.

That someone is this book.

A little TaterTot to sit with your child.

A little TaterTot to help start conversations.

A little TaterTot that extends the hand of love through her message: You Matter.

A TaterTot that will sit with your child and help them feel a little less alone. A little less afraid. And a little more in understanding, 'It's okay to not be okay.'

It's about reaching the eighth grader before they carry that rejection for decades.

For Parents: "What if we could reach our kids in their first heartbreak moment - when they're protecting us from their pain because they love us too much to let us carry it with them?"

This book isn't just healing current wounds - it's my hope to preventing future ones.

Every book that reaches a kid is potentially saving them from 20 years of: "Do I matter?" thoughts.

It's what I needed.


## The Movement - Extending Hands of Hope


As I sit here with you zooming out on the big picture. Sharing my story with you. Can I make a difference with you? Can I be your Trista? Can you allow me to be your friend that can sit with you?

To tell you I understand how it hurts.

To tell you I feel you when you ask those questions.

To tell you that you are allowed to not be okay.

To tell you that you matter. You are enough. You do belong.

You are needed.

To give you a hope, a hand, and a place to sit...

Can I be your Trista in this?

Yes, the book expert told me that the book is meant to be for kids. I do agree. It was what I needed when I didn't understand the emotions and was too afraid to be labeled.

But I also believe what else the expert said, that as the adult reads it with their child that it will also heal the childhood wound that happened.

I carried my pain, alone. The book expert said that it will help others not carry their pain alone.

Not to fix, but to give permission to name it what it is. Much like Keith shared about the waves. Naming them as they are what they are doing what they do.

That crash that hits the foundation, my hope is that the book helps you keep the light shining bright.

The waves and pain are what they are. They will do what they will do.

And when the waters seem calm, one will sneak in and try to flip you upside down.

It's what happens.

And you in this, it's what happens to you.

But I see you in all of this, much as I see myself in what my life has been.

Whether you are six, sixteen, thirty or sixty. We can't prevent the waves from happening. But we can give ourselves permission to be what we are while allowing the waves to do what they do.

This is **The Mz Cookie You Matter Movement.**

This is my mission, my purpose and my hope.

A movement that started with one simple gesture in my life. A hand extended, a hand of hope.

A hand to tell me in my moment I mattered.

My give it one more day, Trista moment.

Now...

A hand to tell someone how much they matter.

Whether you need a Trista or are the Trista for someone...

Here's what I know: Sometimes the smallest gesture - a paid meal, a book, a note that says "someone noticed you today" - can be the hand that pulls someone back from their lowest moment.

I had that moment from Trista. Her invitation to me. To include me, to tell me "I see you, you matter."

Can we do this for someone else? A friend. A stranger. A neighbor. A coworker.

How do we extend the hand of hope to someone?

When you're out to eat, pay for someone else's meal. Include a copy of "***You're Not Too Much; You Matter**"* with a simple note: "Someone saw you today. You matter. When you're ready, pass it forward."

Give one to your server too.

We're not trying to fix anyone.

We're just trying to be Trista.

The person who extends a hand when someone needs to know they're seen.

Hurt people hurt people. But hurt people can heal people.

Even when we're carrying our own pain, we can still reach out and remind someone else they matter.

## The Deeper Why - For the Four I've Lost

I've lost 4 now. Four friends.

Four people I've known that I didn't know where they were at in their emotions. And they made a permanent decision.

As of writing this, my heart feels a pain also when I hear how many veterans we are losing every day. And I wonder. Do they know how much they matter?

When they were in eighth grade, did they have a wound that started to grow? Where they felt alone in pain and no one to sit with them?

What happened that made the wound grow deeper? Was it rejection? Shame? Grief or anger? Feeling used? Being ignored and left out? Dealing with the backlash of someone being jealous?

I wonder, did they experience the same pain as I did and not know how to sit in it? Much like I didn't know how to sit in it?

Did they not want to reach out for help because of being labeled? I was afraid of being labeled yet I was crying for help.

Is there a way we can extend the hope to heal without the label?

Do they have a Trista? Can I be their Trista, extending a hand or a word "I see you."

Not only for this young man in the ER, yet for everyone. Everyone that doesn't want to be labeled. Everyone that isolates and sits in their pain, needing a healing hand. Can I see them where they are, without giving them a label for life?

I think about the four I have lost.

I think about my own moments.

And I wonder.

If there could be a source to help that doesn't tie a label to a moment of emotions one is feeling at the moment. A moment that turns into days and then years because being labeled, that's the painful part.

What if there was something out there that doesn't label a person for life because they are having a moment?

But I believe there's another way.

A way to sit with someone in their darkest moment without labels, without judgment, without shame. A way to stretch out a hand and say: "You are not too much. You matter."

This is why this book exists. This is why this movement exists.

This is my Trista moment...

For the kids carrying wounds.

For the adults silently screaming.

For the veterans who gave us everything yet wonder if anyone cares if they're gone.

The **Mz Cookie You Matter Movement** is here to say: You matter. Your story matters. Your life matters.

Without the labels.

Without the judgment for a life sentence, "You're broken."

And if all you can do today is give it one more day — that's enough.

We'll sit with you in the mud until you can rise.

Without labeling you.

Without telling you to listen.

With giving you space to feel what you feel.

It's okay to feel what you feel. It's okay to have a day where everything is upside down. It's okay to hurt.

And it's also okay to give it one more day.

It's also okay for me to whisper in your heart, "Hey friend, I'm here with you. Not to fix you, yet to tell you. To remind you. You matter. I will notice if you're not here. I will tell you that it's okay to hurt. And I will remind you, that your hurt doesn't define you. It's a hurt, it's a moment and I will not give you a life sentence of labeling you in your moment. You matter to me and these pages let you see."

## The Truth About Healing

Here's what I know about getting this into the world:

I need to start exactly where I am. Raw and real and unpolished. Because the people who need this message most aren't looking for perfection - they're looking for truth. They're looking for someone who gets it. For someone to say, I see you, and I am with you.

That's what I needed.

I didn't reach out and find the help because I didn't trust when someone said, "You'll be fine."

Um.. I'm not fine right now, how do you know I'll be fine?

I needed someone to see me, not fix me.

I needed someone to sit with me instead of trying to hurry my feelings up.

The truth I share… instead of saying "You'll be fine" I say – things will be different.

Instead of "things will get better" I say – things will be different.

One more day. That's all anyone needs sometimes.

Just the permission to hurt today without fixing it, without being strong, without being okay. Just the knowledge that someone sees them in their mess and says "**You matter. Even like this. Especially like this**."

In a world that demands we be okay, I'm giving people permission to not be.

That's the hand I'm extending.

That's the gift from the TaterTot.

The message from the pages of *You're Not Too Much; You matter*.

That is the **Mz Cookie You Matter Movement.**

## The Full Circle - Generational Healing

The Full Circle: •Kids get the book when they need it most •They grow up knowing they matter •They become the adults who pay for strangers' meals •They give books to other kids •The cycle of healing instead of hurting.

The TaterTot just becomes the bridge between: •The eighth

grader who needed someone to sit with them •The adult who finds healing •The future kids who won't have to carry those wounds alone •The parents who are watching helplessly from the sidelines.

This isn't just a book or a movement.

This is generational healing.

This is changing the trajectory of how we handle emotional wounds.

The restaurant thing?

That's just the beginning. Schools, libraries, pediatric offices, anywhere a kid might be sitting with a shattered heart, wondering what's wrong with them.

This book isn't just extending a hand – it's extending a lifeline backwards and forwards through time.

I wonder about that one, sitting amongst their friends, silent. I wonder, do they carry a pain and a wound from when they were in eighth grade like I did. A wound that grows heavier as life happens.

My heart is hurting because I can see what others can't or won't acknowledge - that we're all walking around pretending while drowning inside.

I've lived in that space, I've survived it, and now I can see it more it in strangers' eyes at restaurants, in kids pulling away from their parents, in that young man begging just to be heard.

How do I see it? Because I did it.

I carried the mask. I carried the weight. I isolated and didn't reach out for help.

I see it because I did it.

Because I did it, I want to keep others from sitting in that place alone.

It's heavy enough holding the pain, but doing it alone...I don't want them to do it alone.

## Final Thoughts - You Are the Light

The four friends I've lost - they're part of every book I give away now. They're the reason someone else gets to choose "one more day" instead of a permanent solution to the pain.

A pain, the wound, that life filters through.

I want to give them a voice.

**The Mz Cookie You Matter Movement** isn't just saying "You matter" - it's proving it by showing up without conditions, without paperwork, without making their pain their permanent story.

It's turning everyone that says, "I just needed you to listen. I needed to talk. Now I'm labeled for life" into a mission of purpose.

Give someone one more day. One more reason to stay. Because they matter. Because you matter. Because we all matter.

Just as Trista did for me when I was at my lowest. Her invite helped pull me out. I felt like I mattered to someone in that moment.

You are the lighthouse.

The waves that crash against you—they shaped you, but they don't define you.

Your pain is real. Your hurt is heavy. And you matter—not despite your struggles, but including them.

If you're wearing a mask right now, if you're hiding your pain, if you're sitting in that corner pretending to smile—I see you. I was you.

You're allowed to not be okay.

Your moment doesn't define your lifetime.

And maybe, just maybe, you can be someone else's Trista. Maybe you can extend a hand, offer a simple kindness, sit with someone in their pain without trying to fix them.

Because hurt people hurt people. But healed people can heal people.

Join us. Extend the hand. Pass the hope forward.

And the light you carry—that light matters more than you know.

Keep shining.

You Matter to me, and I matter in this...

# How To

## The Mz.Cookie You Matter Movement

I feel your questions: How do I do this?

I'm asking myself the same questions to this **Mz Cookie You Matter Movement**

This is one way we can join together.

How can we give someone one more day, without fixing, but to tell them:
   **"I see you, you matter."**

One meal. One book. One hand extended.

# The Mz Cookie You Matter Movement

For the kids carrying wounds. For the adults silently screaming. For the veterans who gave us everything yet wonder if anyone cares.

We're here to say: **You matter. Your story matters. Your life matters.**

Without labels. Without judgment. Without making your moment your permanent story.

Here's how it works, and it's beautifully simple:

Order extra copies from Amazon of the book:
 *You're Not Too Much; You Matter*
 (you can search for it by "Mz Cookie You Matter") Author Jen Weiland

**When you're out to eat, pay for someone else's meal. Include a copy of my book with a note:** *"Someone noticed you today. You matter. When you're ready, pass it forward."*

Give one to your server too.

We're not trying to fix anyone. We're just trying to be Trista - the person who extends a hand when someone needs to know they're seen.

Right now, someone is sitting alone, carrying a hurt they can't name. Maybe it's the person at table six picking at their food. Maybe it's the server checking her phone. Maybe it's you.

Sometimes the smallest gesture - a paid meal, a book, **a note that says "someone noticed you today"** - can be the hand that pulls someone back from their lowest moment.

In a world that demands we be okay, I'm giving people permission to not be okay.

Permission to hurt without shame. Permission to feel without being labeled. Permission to have one more day.

Because that's all anyone needs sometimes - just one more day. Just the knowledge that someone sees them in their mess and says: **"You matter. Even like this. Especially like this."**

My four friends are part of every book I give away now. They're the reason someone else gets to choose "one more day" instead of a permanent solution to temporary pain.

The young man in that emergency room is why I refuse to stay silent.

Trista's simple invitation is why I know the smallest gestures can save lives. She saved my life.

So I'm asking you: Will you join this movement?

Will you be someone's Trista?

Will you extend a hand and remind someone they matter?

Because hurt people can heal people.

**Because sometimes the smallest gesture saves a life.**

Because everyone - **EVERYONE** - deserves to know they matter.

Give someone one more day. One more reason to stay.

**Because they matter. Because you matter. Because we all matter.**

Thank you.

As we grow in this, feel free to share your Trista moment with us. Whether you're in a bar, a restaurant, a sporting event, a festival… reach out to someone who needs to know they matter, you see them and it matters to give it one more day.

Let us celebrate you for making a difference. It matters.

*#MzCookieYouMatterMovement* at www.mzcookie.com
*One meal. One book. One hand extended.*

www.mzcookie.com

# The Book for the Mission

Now you're wondering.

Where do I find the book so I can be a part of the **Mz Cookie You Matter Movement?**

The book in paperback is available on Amazon. As we grow this opportunity to be a hand to that quiet one, we hope to have the books in other places. I will update this section as this grows.

Yet for now, you can get the book on your Amazon store.
    Order extra copies or mail one to a friend.
    You don't have to know where they are at, just tell them **They Matter.**

The link is
    https://a.co/d/33Rzm1c

Or if that does not work search:
    **Mz Cookie You Matter** in the search box on Amazon.

I'm not a tech wiz and doing this tech stuff by the seat of my pants. Forgive me for the errors, yet I do know that on the

Amazon search, you will find the book.

You can follow the story as we grow also on my website:
at www.mzcookie.com
Join the newsletter where I will share and celebrate you.
Together, we can give them one more day.

## Can I share one more thing with you?

I want to thank you for being a part of making a difference in someone's life. We don't need to know where someone is in their emotions, yet to know they carry a story inside.

And sometimes those emotions are heavy.

And if we can save them from making a permanent decision and letting them know They Matter, that gives me hope.

Hope we can all be a Trista and change someone's life.

Hope that we can reach them where they are at, not to fix them yet to sit with them.

Hurt people hurt people, yet hurt people heal people.

Follow how we can make a difference at https://mzcookie.com

If you are sitting in a hurt... can I speak to your heart. Gently.

I see you. I feel you. And I know…it hurts, it's suffocating…but you don't have to be in it alone. I'm with you, not to fix, yet to tell you - it's okay to not be okay. Give yourself permission to just be. Don't hurry it up. One day it will be different, not better… just different. You matter to me, and I see you. I was you.

www.mzcookie.com

# Thank You

The biggest thank you to my husband, Tom. Thank you for the support in all of this.

The bigger thank you to Keith Guyll. You sat with me while I was in this journey and you gave me a place to be. Thank you for your wisdom and for seeing me where I was at. Without fixing me, yet guiding me. I am thankful for you beyond words. And thank you for seeing where I was headed before I did.

To all of those that are a part of my story, a story built with many layers of joy and pain.

To Trista... As I have sat with this message in my heart, I want to thank you for reaching me when I was at my lowest point. Your kindness pulled me out and yet I didn't realize it until recently how the bigger picture was shaped by what you did for me. I hope I can honor you to be as you are to others in my own life. Thank you. Nothing is ever random.

# About the Author

### A Little Bit About Mz. Cookie (Jen Weiland)

Mz. Cookie is a professional feeler of feelings.

Not much of an expert on how to heal those things. She knows more about what they feel like.

And they feel messy. And muddy.

Because feelings flip everything upside down— but not in a delicious way like a Pineapple Upside-Down Cake.

Most days, the feelings feel "normal."
    Until one sneaks in—the kind where you're trying to stab water with a fork.

Where the mud gets thick and wants to pull you under.
    Where it's hard to breathe.

Where you don't know much of anything, except that you're sitting there with the feelings.

You know that place—the emotional mud of life.
    You just... **feel.**
    Those feels are real.
    And when you try to stuff them down?

Well, Mz. Cookie can tell you exactly what happens when you do that.
    (Spoiler alert: it doesn't go away—and she's got a few stories to prove it.)

So please.
    Stop stuffing.
    Just let yourself feel.
    You're allowed.

Mz. Cookie is giving you permission.
    She doesn't have a therapist title—more of an unofficial-official title: **Friend.**
    **YOUR friend.**

She believes in therapy—she's been to a few, and she knows how much they help.

So if you're feeling like you want to harm yourself—please, please go to your local ER.
    They do care for you. They will take care of you.

Talk to someone before making a permanent decision.

**Give it one more day.**

**Your life is precious.**
 **You are needed.**

The words in this book are shared to help you know you're not alone.
 That someone knows what it's like.
 That there is a friend willing to sit with you in the mud.
 Not to push you to heal.
 Just to sit in the feels.

Because feeling alone—and not understanding what you're feeling—is hard.
 But you don't have to do it by yourself.
 You have a friend.

**Your friend knows you matter.**
 **Mz. Cookie hopes you see that.**

And when the world feels far away, it helps to have someone beside you who simply says,
 **"Same."**

Not someone needing you to fix it. Just someone being with you.

**With YOU.**
 **That matters**.

**You are seen. You are valued. You are needed.**

**You matter.**

Sign up for Mz Cookie Newsletter at www.mzcookie.com

**You can connect with me on:**
🌐 https://mzcookie.com

# Also by Jen Weiland

**You're Not Too Much; You Matter**
**The book that helps you talk about the hard feelings without lectures or pressure.**

When your child is struggling with big emotions and you don't know what to say, these gentle stories create space for healing conversations

Join Mary the TaterTot and her friends as
they navigate:

Feeling left out and different

Dealing with disappointment and failure

Finding courage when you're scared

Learning that your sensitivity is a gift

Perfect for sensitive children ages 6-16 and the parents who love them

"These aren't just children's stories - they're family healing tools." - Parent review

More at mzcookie.com